By looking at art with children, you can help them develop their innate capacities for careful observation and creative imagination. *People* focuses on portraits and other pictures of people. You'll find a wide range of expressions, gestures, poses, and settings. Children can begin by naming different things they see. You can ask them how they recognize these things, and how each thing might relate to their own lives. You can also lead children to see more elements in each picture, and encourage them to imagine stories based on what their eyes tell them. There are notes at the back of the book to help.

Enjoy looking together!

WITHDRAWN

PROPERTY OF
ONONDAGA COUNTY PUBLIC LIBRARY
"Whoever wilfully detains any . . . property belonging to any public or incorporated library . . . for thirty days after notice in writing to return the same . . . shall be punished by a fine not less than one nor more than twenty-five dollars, or by imprisonment in jail not exceeding six months . . ."

N Y S Education Law
Section 265

ONONDAGA COUNTY
PUBLIC LIBRARY

The Galleries of Syracuse
447 S. Salina St.
Syracuse, NY 13202-2494

ONONDAGA COUNTY PUBLIC LIBRARY
SYRACUSE. NY 13202-2494
YENAWINE, PHILIP   08/02/94
PEOPLE
(4) 1993 J 701.1 YEN
0124 04 485725 01 6   (IC=1)

B012404485725016B

W9-CMQ-642

People

Philip Yenawine

The Museum of Modern Art, New York
Delacorte Press

Acknowledgments
This book was enriched by the contributions of Jessica Altholz,
Amelia Arenas, Harriet S. Bee, Riva Castleman, Peter Galassi, David Gale,
Abigail Housen, Nancy Miller, Carol Morgan, and the designers
Takaaki Matsumoto, Michael McGinn, and Mikio Sakai of M Plus M
Incorporated. I would also like to acknowledge Osa Brown,
Mikki Carpenter, Penny Cooper, Matthew Diehl, Barbara Greenberg,
George Nicholson, Edward Robinson, Rena Rosenwasser, Marc Sapir,
Richard Tooke, and Rebecca, Tad, and Patricia Yenawine. I am extremely
grateful to all of them.

Copyright ©1993 by The Museum of Modern Art, New York

All rights reserved. No part of this book may be reproduced or transmitted
in any form or by any means, electronic or mechanical, including photo-
copying, recording, or by any information storage and retrieval system,
without the written permission of the publishers, except where permitted
by law.

Picture reproduction rights, where relevant, reserved by S.P.A.D.E.M. and
A.D.A.G.P., Paris.

The trademark Delacorte Press® is registered in the U.S. Patent and
Trademark Office.

Library of Congress Cataloging in Publication Data

Yenawine, Philip.
People/Philip Yenawine.
p.   cm.
Includes index.
Summary: Examines, in simple terms, the meaning of various portraits and
other pictures of people at The Museum of Modern Art.
1. Humans in art—Juvenile literature. 2. Art appreciation—Juvenile
literature. 3. The Museum of Modern Art (New York, N.Y.)—Juvenile
literature. [1. Humans in art. 2. Art appreciation. 3. The Museum of
Modern Art (New York, N.Y.)] I. Title.
N7625.5.Y46 1993
701'.1—dc20
92-11203
CIP
AC
ISBN 0-87070-174-6 (MoMA)
ISBN 0-385-30901-5 (Delacorte Press)

The Museum of Modern Art
11 West 53 Street
New York, NY 10019

Delacorte Press
Bantam Doubleday Dell Publishing Group, Inc.
1540 Broadway
New York, NY 10036

Printed in Italy

October 1993
10   9   8   7   6   5   4   3   2   1

Artists make pictures of people.

Pablo Picasso. *Woman with a Flowered Hat.* 1921

Many pictures tell stories. A story can be about someone who is thoughtful and serious . . .

Paul Cézanne. *Boy in a Red Waistcoat.* 1893–95

or about a person who is slightly silly. Why, do you think, is this girl smiling?

Fernando Botero. *Mona Lisa, Age Twelve*. 1959

People can be doing things. What is going on in this picture?

Hilaire-Germain-Edgar Degas. *Two Dancers*. 1905

4

Or people can just be together. What can you tell about these two?

Balthus. *Joan Miró and His Daughter Dolores*. 1937–38

Sometimes you have to look hard because there are so many people to see.

Honoré Sharrer. *Workers and Paintings.* 1943, dated 1944

Find all the children.

Sometimes you have to use your eyes *and* your imagination!

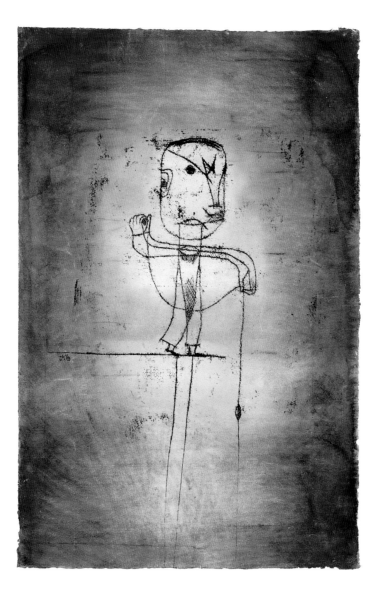

Paul Klee. *The Angler.* 1921

Could you ever imagine that these were the same man?

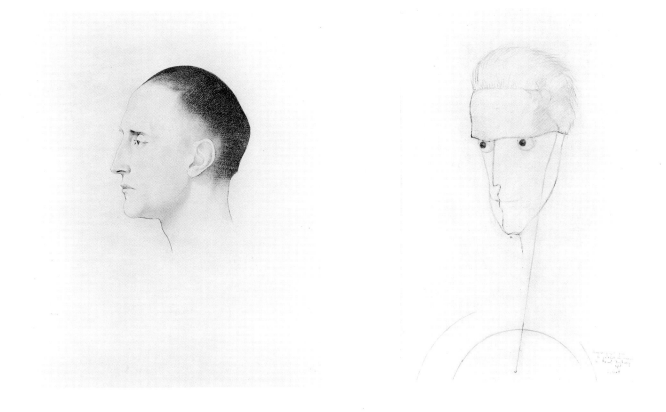

Joseph Stella. *Marcel Duchamp.* c. 1920; Jean Crotti. *Marcel Duchamp.* 1915

Guess what each of these children is doing.

Can you tell where they live?

Helen Levitt. Untitled. 1972–74

What about these warmly dressed people?

Can you guess what each might be looking at?

Ben Shahn. *Willis Avenue Bridge*. 1940

Can you tell how this woman feels by the look on her face?

What do you think she is doing?

Hilaire-Germain-Edgar Degas. *At the Milliner's.* c. 1882

Look at each of these expressions. What feeling do you think each one describes?

Lovis Corinth. *Self-Portraits.* 1902

Can you learn about people from looking at their eyes?

Guess what these young people are thinking.

Lucian Freud. *Girl with Leaves.* 1948

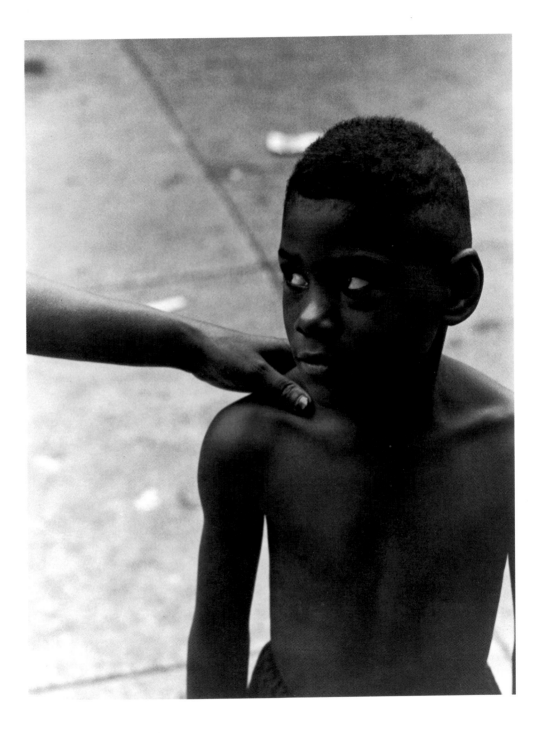

Roy DeCarava. *Boy.* 1952

Look at how these people sit. Do you think they like having their picture painted?

How can you tell?

Alice Neel. *Benny and Mary Ellen Andrews.* 1972

What can you learn from looking at the faces and hands of these people?

Oskar Kokoschka. *Hans Tietze and Erica Tietze-Conrat.* 1909

Edouard Vuillard. *Mother and Sister of the Artist.* c. 1893

Look at the woman sitting down.

What can you tell about her from the expression on her face?

Now look at the other one.

Can you guess what she is like by the way she is standing?

This picture gives you a lot to look at.

Who are these people?

What are they holding?

Why is that man on the ground?

Make up a story about these people.

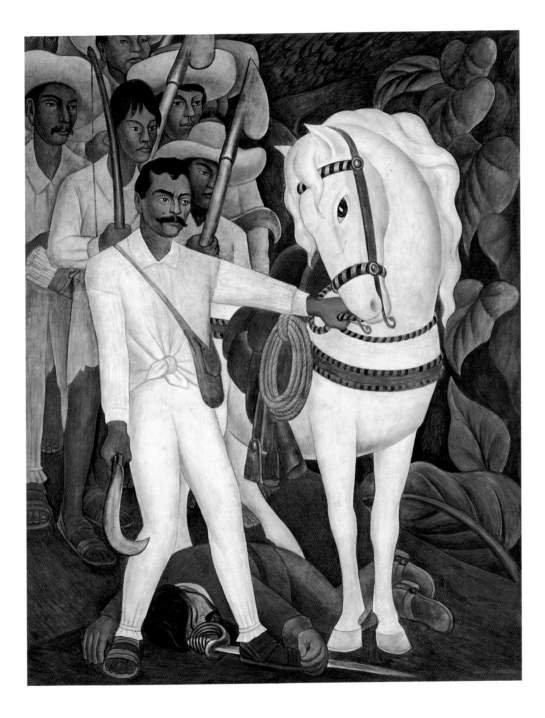

Diego Rivera. *Agrarian Leader Zapata.* 1931

Now it's time for you to draw pictures of people. Can you make young and old ones? Can you make them happy or serious? Can you draw them doing things? Can you make a mystery? How many ways can you draw yourself?

The art in this book is in the collection of The Museum of Modern Art in New York City, but you can find interesting pictures at any museum or gallery. You can also look for pictures and patterns in magazines, books, buildings, parks, and gardens.

Page 1

Pablo Picasso
Woman with a Flowered Hat. 1921
Pastel on paper
25 1/4 x 19 1/2" (64 x 49.5 cm)
Gift of Jacqueline Picasso

Picasso used brightly colored pastels to make this serene-faced woman. Her eyes, nose, and brow might make us think of a figure cut from stone, maybe even a classical goddess. Her hat and collar, however, make her more peasant-like. Perhaps Picasso wanted us to relate the two.

Page 2

Paul Cézanne
Boy in a Red Waistcoat. 1893–95
Oil on canvas
32 x 25 5/8" (81.2 x 65 cm)
Fractional gift of Mr. and Mrs. David Rockefeller (the donors retaining a life interest in the remainder)

This boy's relaxed, slouching pose contrasts with the sharp intelligence of his wide-eyed gaze. You might also point out the rich quality of Cézanne's paint here.

Page 3

Fernando Botero
Mona Lisa, Age Twelve. 1959
Oil and tempera on canvas
6' 11 1/8" x 6' 5" (211 x 195.5 cm)
Inter-American Fund

It is not necessary to know da Vinci's *Mona Lisa* to appreciate the humor in the wide grin of this mischievous miss.

Page 4

Hilaire-Germain-Edgar Degas
Two Dancers. 1905
Charcoal and pastel on tracing paper, mounted on wove paper
43 x 32" (109.3 x 81.2 cm)
The William S. Paley Collection

Degas's deceptively simple studies of dancers are not always clearly readable. Where are these two? Are they sitting or standing? The dancer in front is probably fixing her toe shoe, but what about the other one?

Page 5

Balthus
(Baltusz Klossowski de Rola)
Joan Miró and His Daughter Dolores. 1937–38
Oil on canvas
51 1/4 x 35" (130.2 x 88.9 cm)
Abby Aldrich Rockefeller Fund

The artist Joan Miró and his daughter are posed rather stiffly, yet the way Miró holds the child and the way she leans against him suggest warmth and trust. Note how little background detail there is, as in Degas's *Two Dancers.*

Pages 6–7

Honoré Sharrer
Workers and Paintings. 1943, dated 1944 (Detail)
Oil on composition board
11 5/8 x 37" (29.5 x 94 cm)
Gift of Lincoln Kirstein

Against an urban backdrop, the artist depicts several family groupings, each holding a painting. Look at the variety of expressions and gestures to see what is going on.

Paul Klee
The Angler. 1921
Watercolor, transfer drawing, and pen and ink on paper, mounted on cardboard
20 x 12 5/8" (50.6 x 31.9 cm)
John S. Newberry Collection

Klee's drawings often resemble children's, in that they are simple, playful, and imaginative. This means the viewer must think creatively to figure them out. For example, how many different faces exist here?

Joseph Stella
Marcel Duchamp. c. 1920
Silverpoint
27 1/4 x 21" (69.2 x 53.3 cm)
Katherine S. Dreier Bequest

Does this careful drawing, contemplative in pose and mood, tell us much about the subject, artist Marcel Duchamp? Can you be certain of his age? his personality? Compare his hairline, brow, nose, mouth, and chin to those parts in the next image.

Jean Crotti
Marcel Duchamp. 1915
Pencil
21 1/2 x 13 1/2" (54.5 x 34.3 cm)
Purchase

In this drawing, almost a caricature, Duchamp's eyes are made to seem particularly intense, and his brow is stronger than in the other picture. Ask children to list all the things they might guess about this one man from the two representations of him.

Helen Levitt
Untitled. 1972–74
Dye-transfer print
9 1/4 x 14 1/4" (23.6 x 36.3 cm)
The Gilman Foundation Fund

These city children are all caught up in some activity. Though they are near one another, they are not really interacting. Each seems to set his or her own mood.

Ben Shahn
Willis Avenue Bridge. 1940
Tempera on paper over composition board
23 x 31 3/8" (58.4 x 79.7 cm)
Gift of Lincoln Kirstein

The alert eyes of the woman on the right could signal many things, from suspicion to watching for a bus. Don't miss the long white gown on the figure on the left. The diagonals call to mind the structure of a bridge, and you can recognize water beyond.

Hilaire-Germain-Edgar Degas
At the Milliner's. c. 1882
Pastel on paper
27 5/8 x 27 3/4" (70.2 x 70.5 cm)
Gift of Mrs. David M. Levy

This sweet-faced woman seems pleased with the hat she has tried on. Many things are left out of this picture, such as the mirror into which she is probably looking.

Lovis Corinth
Self-Portraits. 1902
Pencil
18 3/8 x 12 1/4" (47.7 x 31.1 cm)
Gift of The Lauder Foundation and by exchange

Look carefully at each face to see how the artist changes his eyes, and the different ways he shapes his mouth. Looking into a mirror and imitating the expressions might make it easier to talk about the moods set by each.

Lucian Freud
Girl with Leaves. 1948
Pastel on gray paper
18 7/8 x 16 1/2" (47.9 x 41.9 cm)
Purchase

Consider what this young girl might be staring at so steadfastly, and also where she could be, given the leaves above her.